Walk With Me

Dedication

This book is dedicated to my two precious grandchildren, Trysten and Kayden. You have made my world so much more beautiful by being in it. I love you.

Table of Contents

Walk With Me

Walk with me, come take my hand, fear not my precious one

This road of life we walk along begins like the rising sun.

As sure as the sun rises, it will set to end each day

The night will come, the stars will shine, the moon will light your way.

Your path at times may seem like you're never quite on track

Just don't let go, hold on tight, I'll always have your back.

I promise you, believe in me, when you're tired you'll make it through.

I'll guide you, I will stand by you in everything you do.

Have faith in me, my love for you is everlasting to eternity.

Hand in hand please don't fear, just come and walk with me.

Anna Lachman

If

If heaven were gold and the skies woven lace

If the stars were all diamonds and the moon had a face.

If the sun could warm hearts and the rain soothe your woes

If the snow were your friend and your heart was a rose.

If the grass was your blanket and the trees danced with glee

If the wind was your angel and the sea was your tea.

If sparrows were souls of those we held dear

We'd know when we're gone there is nothing to fear.

If life feels too short and the days seem too long

If life drags you down and things all go wrong.

If you can believe that there's hope faith and love

Then you have found home - it's in Him, God above.

Lost

I wish I were lost somewhere in an ancient forest

Far away from the hustle and bustle of this busy world.

With pines towering and stretching above me for as far as the eye can see.

And piercing through the giant boughs

Are rays of sunshine that filter down upon me.

As I gaze upwards, I feel a slight breeze brush my cheek

And the scent of wild roses and lilies greet me.

The sights and sounds of birds, many unknown to me, but oh so beautiful

Is music to my ears and fills my eyes with wonder.

I inhale a deep breath, I smile as I stand perfectly still

In this ancient place of greenery and beauty.

Tiny brooks trickle, and waterfalls cascade down jagged rocks

That jut out of the side of the mountain.

A blanket of fern covers the ground

But also drapes magnificent boughs, soft, cushiony,

Probably a place for many animals to make a comfortable bed.

Oh, what a breathtaking place to be standing in the middle of.

Away from all the stresses of the world

So close to God, so surrounded by peace.

Mom

If I heard your voice a thousand times in just one day

It would never be enough.

You have enriched my life beyond words.

Every minute of every day I am thankful for you.

Your love is unwavering

You are graceful, compassionate and kind.

You are giving and forgiving, you are non judgemental.

Your eyes sparkle, the windows to your beautiful soul.

Your touch is that of an angel.

Your voice is soft, gentle, and calming.

I feel healed and safe when I am with you.

You are my sanctuary.

I feel comfort and warmth knowing you are there.

You are with me in my darkest hours

As well as through my triumphs.

You are my best friend.

I embrace you, I am blessed.

Your beauty grows with every passing day.

You are a gift from God.

"I'm eternally grateful for you, my precious Mom."

Lost Love

It was late in August, a clear warm night.

Did we meet by chance or fate?

She was all alone as she walked on by

Then she stopped as if to wait.

My eyes met hers as she turned to me

With a smile she said "Hello."

I felt as though her soul reached out to mine,

A friend from long ago?

A tiny woman, small in frame

Hair etched with shades of grey.

Her eyes of blue, so mournful,

So sad and far away.

I felt compelled to talk with her

A feeling I can't explain.

What happened to this precious soul?

Her eyes welled up with pain.

"It's been two years," she whispered,

"Since God took my love from me

I wander lost, in search of him

So I may too be free."

I took her hands and held them tight

I prayed "Lord, ease her grief,

Comfort her and give her peace,

From this burden send relief."

I felt a warmth even though the night set in,

I knew God heard my prayer.

She smiled at me and said goodbye,

And in an instant she wasn't there.

"Tis better to have loved and lost than to never have loved at all."

- Alfred Lord Tennyson

Home

I love my home, my treasure chest

For all who've entered I am blessed.

Family and friends have graced these walls

Laughter and love have filled the halls.

When all is silent and I'm alone

I feel such peace here in my home.

Every day when I awake

There's nothing for granted that I take.

Who could ask for anything more?

God bless all who walk through my door.

Anna Lachman

Seen But Not Heard

There's no pain greater than to be seen but not heard.

To be heard only to be hurt,

To be hurt and have to hear "I'm sorry."

To hear "I'm sorry," with hollow meaning

When every hollow meaning has taken away

Another God given moment forever.

Be kind, listen, forgive, love.

The Sky

It envelopes and blankets the entire earth

From the beginning of time it was given birth.

Sometimes blue, with the sun a glare

So bright it gives life to everything everywhere.

Clouds bring rain and water the ground

Plants and trees grow abound.

And when the sun goes down and night sets in

Is when the light show starts to begin.

The moon rises high and the stars shine bright

It's breathtaking to watch, a beautiful sight.

The sky is one of God's amazing creations

From each corner of the world, across all nations.

"Everything has beauty but not everyone sees it."

Anna Lachman

You Can Do Anything

Don't ever give up on your goals, wishes, or dreams

You can do anything, it's not as far-fetched as it seems.

Shoot for the stars, reach for the moon and dance out in the rain

You never know if you'll ever get a chance to do it again.

Take that leap of faith, you might be surprised where you land.

And if you fall, don't give up, back on your feet you'll stand.

Don't feel that you're not good enough because you truly are.

With courage and determination forge ahead, you will go far.

There may be blows along the way but stronger you will be

For every blow along the way much clearer you will see.

You were put here on this earth, God will teach you every day

Through trials and tribulations, you will surely find your way.

So live your life to the fullest, make all your dreams come true.

You are special, you are loved,

And you can do anything you want to do!

"Don't dream your life, live your dreams."

Without You

Where would I be without you in my life?

You're a strong shoulder to cry on.

What would I do without you in my life?

You're my pillar of strength.

Who would be there to brighten my days?

You are my sunshine, my love and my best friend.

Where would I be without you?

Fear

Don't let it get inside of your head
Or crawl under the sheets with you.
Don't open the door and invite it in
You'll do things you'd normally not do.

You'll question your abilities -
What is wrong and what is right?
Sleep will elude you, panic sets in
As the shadows surround you at night.

Somewhere, somehow, I lost it
There was a time I was so strong.
I got weary of the daily grind
It's here where things went wrong.

The evil waits in the shadows and taunts,
"Come and follow me,
You'll have all the riches in the world
Close the door and you will see."

Just then I hear a familiar voice
"It is fear that's gripped you so.
Don't let it fool you, remember your faith
Push back, it will have to go."

I felt a warmth rush through my soul
My faith was pushing it back.
Then the door closed behind it
As it faded back into the black.

Walk With Me

Peace returned, I could breathe again
The fear had lifted, the demons had gone.
I felt renewed, so much lighter now
No more terror in the night, just calm.

"Fear is the thief of dreams."

While She Lies Sleeping

I wonder about times when I was not yet here,
About her forgotten loves.
My only fear is that she'll think I'm the same, not loyal, untrue.
I whisper her name and so softly "I love you"
While she lies sleeping.

I know she's been hurt, past loves let her down,
And I want her to know I'll always be around.
Just let me in, please open your heart
I whisper her name and so softly "I love you"
While she lies sleeping.

I want her to know it's only her that I love,
Love so fresh and new sent from heaven above.
As I lie here beside her and watch her gently breathe
I whisper her name and so softly "I love you"
While she lies sleeping.

I touch her soft beauty, my eyes warm with tears
I want no other partner, only you, always near.
My sleeping beauty, my eyes will never stray
I whisper her name and so softly "I love you"
While she lies sleeping.

Whispers

Whispers of evil erupt in the still of night
Whispers of fear as they hold each other tight.

Whispers of men who love the thrill
Whispers of those they're about to kill.

Whispers of men about to go wild
Whispers of women clutching their child.

Whispers of the innocent grow through the night
Whispers of knowing what will come with the light.

Whispers of the gas chamber that will snuff them out
Whispers of the terrified, no one will hear their shouts.

Whispers of ruling a perfect world without them
Whispers of freedom that will never be again.

Whispers heighten as the executioners prepare
Whispers of the innocent as they huddle in despair.

Whispers intensify with the dawn's early light
Whispers continue as they're marched to their plight.

Whispers of "I love you" are heard all down the line
Whispers of "God help us", as the sun begins to shine.

Whispers of the cowards so proud of what they've done
Whispers of each man, woman and child as they die one by one.

Whispers turn to silence in a room once filled with love
Whispers as God carries each soul to heaven up above.

Whispers of the evil and corrupt, elated – their enemy has fallen
But whispers turn to screams when their own souls burn in hell.

"For the dead and the living, we must bear witness."
- Elie Wiesel

This Chance

Goodnight my love, sleep well
May the angels hold you tight
And in the morning when you wake
I will be here by your side.

Your friend, your partner, your everything
In me you can confide.
We'll always be open and honest
There is nothing we will hide.

For all our blessed days through good and bad
Whatever unfolds our love will keep us strong.
There will never be a day we can't manage
And never a day too long.

Through adversities and challenges
With God's help we'll handle it all.
Our faith and love will carry us
We may falter but never fall.

We may get weak and tired
As life puts us through the test
So hold me close as I hold you
And together we will heal and rest.

As allies through this walk on earth
We'll stay strong and always true.
For I am blessed to have had this chance
To share my life with you.

"To love and be loved is to feel the sun from both sides."
~David Viscott

Trysten

Even on my darkest days the sun still shines on me

Because of you there will always be light and goodness in my world.

When I am at my weakest you lift me up and keep me strong.

When I feel like crying you make me laugh.

When I am troubled the sound of your voice and laugh

The feel of your hugs, the sparkle in your eyes

Your beautiful smile, erase all worries.

Your kind, gentle spirit and the love in your heart

Are what make you so special.

God has blessed me and given me you,

God's blessings are upon you and the angels in heaven are rejoicing

For you are special, my precious Trysten.

Anna Lachman

HOMELESS

On the corner of the street,

I saw him sitting there,

He lived in a box he called his home,

His feet were worn and bare.

As I approached, his eyes met mine;

His face was gaunt and worn,

He had newspapers for his bed,

And his clothes were ragged and torn.

I could hear the music, from his guitar,

As he played for charity,

A homeless man, in the bitter cold,

He played for you and me.

His hands were cold and trembling,

As he strummed a haunting song,

I wondered what had brought him here?

How life had done him wrong?

As I stood, and watched him softly play,

Many passed him by, uncomfortable,

Or were they guilty?

They couldn't look him in the eye.

He looked at me and softly said,

"Can I play you a special song?"

"Just play me anything", I said,

I knew he couldn't go wrong.

It felt as if he played just for me,

As though no one else was around,

In silence, I stood and watched this man,

His open guitar case lay on the ground.

I placed some coins in his open case,

Walk With Me

In hopes this would help for today,

He thanked me, and I wished him well,

Then I turned and walked away.

Until you walk in someone else's shoes,

Don't judge another man,

Give what you can,

Listen to his song, for him, God has a plan.

What goes around will come around,

Be kind, reach out your hand,

Come together, help those in need,

And we'll all live in a better land.

Being unwanted, unloved, uncared for, forgotten by everybody, I think that is a much greater hunger, a much greater poverty than the person who has nothing to eat.

~ Mother Teresa

Treasures in Heaven

What is life if it is not lived?

Live life to the fullest.

What is happiness?

Be good to yourself and others.

What is sorrow?

Time will heal.

What is anger?

Learn to forgive.

What is fear?

Have faith.

What is friendship?

A shoulder to cry on.

What is wealth?

Give to those in need.

What is nature and animals?

Nurture, protect and be kind.

What is our purpose?

To serve God.

What is our reward?

Treasures in heaven.

Together for Life

No one ever saw him cry

A man of strength and pride.

Who would have known, the sadness he felt,

Was hidden deep inside?

A family man with two small kids,

His soulmate was his wife.

He had it all, he knew that his

Was a perfect life.

Oh yes, there had been hard times,

But together they pulled through.

Their marriage was made in heaven,

They were one, no longer two.

The children were a blessing,

A girl followed by a boy.

Healthy and so beautiful,

His heart was filled with joy.

The children grew, as did his love for them,

His wife, he loved her so.

How could he have known, that the time had come,

For the love of his life to go?

A simple test, she wasn't feeling well,

Probably nothing at all.

She waited for the results to come,

And then she got the call.

That night she broke the news to him
Said she'd fight with all she had.
She reassured him it would be okay,
It really wasn't that bad.

The months went by, the treatments continued
And she seemed to be doing so well.
But the sickness came back with a vengeance,
He wanted to scream and yell.

But he kept all his feelings inside for her sake,
He knew he had to be strong.
His children were young and they'd often ask,
"Daddy, what's wrong with Mom?"

The children were aware that Mommy was tired,
And soon might go away.
To a place where she could rest
A place called heaven, he would say.

He was thankful that the children were young,
For time would heal their pain.
But how could he be both mom and dad?
It would never be the same.

He held her frail body so gently in his arms,
And lovingly stroked her hair.
She kissed him, took a final breath, and then was gone
She was no longer there.

Now standing at her grave
His soul mate gone from his side.

Walk With Me

He cried, this pillar of strength
Shed tears he could no longer hide.

He held the hands of his children,
And in their eyes he saw his wife.
He felt her love and her spirit,
And knew they'd be together for life.

"You never know how strong you are until being strong is the only choice you have."

Anna Lachman

Today

I don't know where I'm going
But I know where I have been.
I know what I've accomplished
And I know what I have seen.

I cannot tell the future
But can live and be thankful for today.
Enjoy every hour I'm given,
And let nothing stand in my way.

There are paths that I have chosen
That weren't always right.
But even when I was lost
I somehow always found the light.

Love conquers all and is so easy to give
This I can control.
This is what it's all about
This is what keeps me whole.

To live is to learn, a student I am,
And by learning I will grow.
There can be many outcomes
You are what you reap, and you are what you sow.

My hand reaches out to those in need
My heart is here for you.
Rest your head upon my shoulder
When you don't know what to do.

Right now, right here, is all we have
Every moment is a gift from above.
Just live each day like it was your last,
And give it all your love.

Anna Lachman

There's a Light

There's no chance life will ever be the same again,
I will never get past this horrific pain.

There are no words that can heal this tragedy,
How I'll carry on I just can't see.

There's no place I can hide, there is no sleep
I cry out for you and forever I'll weep.

There's no sun in the sky, only darkness around
My soul is now lost and will never be found.

There's no reason to laugh or smile or sing
You were my world, my love, my everything.

There's no summer, winter, spring or fall
Without you there are no seasons at all.

There's silence all around me, only memories so true
How can I live when I don't have you?

There are no gentle arms to hold me tight
It just isn't fair, it just isn't right.

There's only one thing that I can do,
Is to pray to the Lord that I'll again see you.

There's so much grief, dear Lord hear my prayer
Let my love know I will always be there.

Walk With Me

There's a light that will come to all one day,

And we will be reunited with those that were taken away.

"To live in hearts we leave behind is not to die."

~Thomas Campbell

Sunshine

Sunshine lights up my life and brightens every day

Bubbling with love and energy and oh so much to say.

Eyes of sparkling blue with hair of pure spun gold

Every day with you is filled with warmth, never a day of cold.

Your face is that of an angel with a spirit as bright as the sun

Full of love and laughter, we always have so much fun.

Satin skin, so perfect, the warmth of your hand in mine

When you lay your head upon my chest it's then that all is fine.

An angel who skips and sings, spreading to all your joy and love

Oh how God must love you as He looks down from heaven above.

So grateful, I am blessed, that you were sent to me

My precious little granddaughter, here for you I'll always be.

"To my beloved Kayden Hope...My joy, my life...my everything"

Spanish Angel

"For Adipel and Jibran"

Where the palm trees sway in the ocean breeze

And the sand is so soft and white

Where the ocean mirrors the clear blue skies

With days so sunny and bright.

This beautiful island in the Caribbean

The Republic of the Dominican

I found her there, in a time of need

An angel and a special friend.

This place, a tropical jewel

As a tourist I was far from home

And when I needed help she was there

I was not alone.

Back in Canada, my native land

I wonder how you are

And though the miles are many

In my heart you are never far.

God's blessings across the miles

To you and your little son

For all the kindness you showed

You are blessed for everyone.

I know your life's not easy

But you're strong and will make it through.

All the good you do each day

Anna Lachman

Will come back to you, it's true.

When I think of you it gives me strength
"Don't worry," you said to me
God will take care of everything
Have faith and you will see."

Where the palm trees sway in the ocean breeze
I'll find you again one day.
A Spanish angel, so warm and kind
In my heart, you're not far away.

Silent Beauty

The snow fell gently today

The fluffy flakes rocking in the whispering breeze.

Down, down, down,

Finally settling into a blanket of white.

The sun peeked through the winter clouds

Reflecting each sparkle and glitter of the white diamonds.

The heavily laden pine and spruce arch their branches

To shoulder the weight of the newly fallen snow.

There, the chickadees and sparrows huddle

Chattering amongst each other for the perfect bough.

And the snow continued throughout the day

Silently falling, beautiful, calm, flawless, breathtaking.

The land shimmered, everything covered in heavenly white.

And the night came as did the moon and the stars.

The snow glistened, sparkled, soft, new and pure.

Untouched and undisturbed for now.

Down, down, down,

Silently floating it cascades into a magical winter wonderland.

Hypnotizing, serene, so peaceful and graceful.

Fresh and new.

My heart is warmed by the beauty of it.

Pray with Me

"Pray with me?" he asked, as I tucked him into bed.

I held his hands and closed my eyes, and then I bowed my head.

His hands so small inside of mine, my gentle little boy

My heart was warmed, it touched me so, I was overwhelmed with joy.

"Watch over us and keep us safe, each and every day,

Thank you for your blessings you've given us today.

Bless us with your presence and calm our daily fears

Guide us in our daily lives, throughout the coming years.

Keep us strong and healthy, with our hearts filled full of love

Send us angels of protection from heaven up above,

Forgive us our sins, we thank you for your grace."

We said "Amen." He smiled at me, and I kissed his precious face.

"For you Trysten..."

My Everything

You're my love, my life, my everything

You make me want to dance and sing.

You're my sunshine on a cloudy day

You take my rainy days away.

You brighten my days with your loving smile

Every day with you is a day worthwhile.

You're my shining star in the sky at night

Your spirit fills up every day with light.

You're the wind on the wings of a butterfly

With you in my life I will never cry.

You're every single glorious sunrise

You are there in the sparkle of my eyes.

You're everything I ever dreamed

My love, my life, my everything.

"If I had my life to live all over again, I would find you sooner so I could love you longer."

Never Touch Ground

Today as I looked into the peaceful blue sky

I felt like a bird just learning to fly.

We must take that big step no more old thoughts, just new

That's the way it must be for me and for you.

So let's shed our old nests, all our fears, our unrest

There's so much for us to do, with you I'll be best.

For your love is the fire that flows through my veins

With you by my side, gone are the pains.

The strongest of loves has its ups and its downs

From this day forward let's never touch ground.

Stop

What will it take for the fighting to cease

For the pain and suffering to stop?

Will you ever get along as friends?

Will your guns you ever drop?

So many innocent people

Have suffered and died in pain.

All the lives the wars have taken

Yet you murder again and again.

Hundreds of years have passed us by

And peace is still nowhere in sight.

Thousands run and hide in fear

But you hunt them day and night.

The babies and the children

They do not stand a chance

Yet, without a thought you pilfer their lives away

Then you rejoice, and laugh and dance.

The elderly, they cannot run

Heads bowed they quietly pray

They hide, they are terrified

But your soldiers steal their lives away.

Horrified, the families mourn and grieve

As you come back again and again

You've destroyed their homes and futures

Anna Lachman

When will it ever end?

The soldiers that we send to war
To protect us night and day
Many so young, they never return
Their lives are snatched away.

There is no race or religion
That rises above the rest
This time we are given upon the earth
Is to be lived as we can best.

God is watching you from His heavenly post
He's disappointed in His human race.
He gave us grace and a second chance
Our lives, and this beautiful place.

So if you want to go home to Him
When your time on earth is done
Put an end to the fighting and the pain
For no war was ever won.

"Bless all of the innocent souls that have lost their lives in the many senseless wars."

Kindness

Kindness is not selfish or proud

It is an act, a gesture

An outstretched hand

Or a shoulder to cry on.

It is unlimited and has no restrictions

It is listening even though you may not understand

It is seeing even though you may be blind.

It is comfort and warmth

It is neither rich nor poor

It has no colour, race, or religion

It doesn't judge, ridicule or hate

It is giving and forgiving

It is a warm hug, a kind word, a smile

It is a door that never closes.

It is nourishment for the soul and heals the heart

It doesn't cost anything and should be given freely

With no expectations of anything in return

It is the one thing that will unite the world and its people.

An act of kindness will never be forgotten

By the One that is most important

And goodness will surround you

All of your days.

"Be kind, for everyone you meet is fighting a hard battle."
~ Ian Maclaren

Anna Lachman

Just a Breath Away

When you hear the distant thunder

Rolling in over the plains

And you smell that familiar scent

So sweet before it rains.

In the glory of each sunrise

As it washes us in light

In the softness of the sunset

In the quiet of the night

The chattering of the sparrows

Happy and so free

The beauty of the flowers

And the busy bumblebee

Pussy willows in the spring

And lilacs mauve and white

Hazy days of summer, fall colours

Such a glorious sight

Winter brings a time of rest

With fireplaces glowing bright.

In every single snowflake

You will see a special light.

Look up towards the heavens in the darkness

And you will see

The stars that sparkle like diamonds

From here to eternity.

The moon casts a glow over the land

A beacon in the night

Its beauty is there for all to see

Truly a breathtaking sight.

Walk With Me

In everything you see

And everything you do

Know that I am never far

I am always close to you.

Our time on earth is priceless

So enjoy each and every day

Heaven is just a breath away, believe in what I say.

Since I left you've been so sad

But it's paradise where I am

So live your life, don't waste it

And I will be here to take your hand.

Anna Lachman

I Waited

I waited for you
For you to come
I waited for you
In the rising sun.

I longed for you
As the sun set down
I waited for you
To come around.

I yearned for you
Every day and night
I hoped you would come
That you just might.

I dreamed of the day
When you'd carry me away
I waited for you
Every single day.

I hoped that you'd love me
As I loved you
I waited for the darkness
To turn to blue.

I ached for your touch
And I prayed for the day
You'd appear there before me
And sweep me away.

Walk With Me

Still here I wait
As the night settles in
Where does it stop
Where does it begin?

My life is not whole
Yet I must carry on
Oh, why didn't you come,
Where have you gone?

As I lie here awake
My heart heavy with pain
I know that it's true
I won't see you again.

I want you to live
And be happy and free
I'll dream of the way
I'd hoped it would be.

I waited so long
And I want you to know
There's a place in my heart
That will never let go.

Anna Lachman

It's Jaci

It's me Mom, it's Jaci,

There's some things I need to say.

I know you miss me terribly

Since I passed that New Year's Day.

I feel your pain and sorrow

And I'm with you when you cry.

It was my time to leave this earth

But it didn't mean goodbye.

I'm with you when you hold my picture

So tight against your chest

At night when you are lying in bed

I'm with you as you rest.

I want you to know I'm all around

In everything you do

In life you were my dear best friend

A mother so warm and true.

I see the way you're raising my son

It makes my spirit glow

I'm right there every step of the way

As I watch my baby grow.

When you're at your lowest

Walk With Me

And you feel you can't go on
Remember I'm in this beautiful place
I'm happy and I'm strong.

This place is truly paradise
There are many loved ones here
I know it's hard to imagine it
But I'm with you, I'm always near.

I'm with you in the mornings
Through the days and every night
I'm in the twinkling of the stars
And the sun's warming light.

I love it when I hear you laugh
And I see you having fun
So be strong for me and carry on
I'm living through my son.

Don't question why this happened
We all must pass one day
There's a thin veil that separates us
Heaven's not far away.

No one knows the day or hour
When our time on earth is done
Live your days to the fullest
God wants you to laugh and have fun.

We'll be together again some day

Anna Lachman

In this glorious other land

And when you come to the other side

I'll be there to take your hand.

"You care so much you feel you will bleed to death with the pain of it."

~ J.K. Rowling

Heaven Gained an Angel

She slowly sat down in her chair
This woman of beauty and style.
Clutching the picture she loved so much
She managed a simple smile.

The years had taken a toll on her
And she had no more strength to fight
Her blue eyes gazed up at the clock
It was nine o'clock at night.

She gently rocked and closed her eyes
With the photo against her chest
It was time she knew
It was time to go
All she wanted to do was rest.

She thought of her dog which had passed away
How she missed her little friend
And all her loved ones, her family and friends
How would they deal with her end?

She sighed and managed another weak smile
Oh, they will be alright
I have to go, it's time for me
And she slipped away into the night.

She crossed the bridge to the other side
She's at peace, there's no more pain

Anna Lachman

And there to greet her is her little dog,

Together once again.

She scoops up her precious little friend

What a glorious, blessed sight

With angels all around them, together again,

They walk into the heavenly light.

"In Loving Memory of Lori"

Golden Years

The years go by so quickly
We don't even realize.
I want you to know, it's always been you
You're the one I idolize.

Life is busy and hectic
Always so much to do
I'm glad I was able to spend
All these precious years with you.

From the first day that I met you
I knew you were the one.
You were my love, my lucky star
My glorious shining sun.

You filled my life with laughter
And brightened every day.
And when my world came crashing down
You took the pain away.

When I was weak you reached out your hand
And held mine so very tight
You lifted the darkness and gave me strength
And filled my life with light.

We climbed every mountain, you and I
And walked in the silky white sand
We traveled through time together
As one in our own special land.

I wouldn't change a single thing
I am because of you
You are the one I dreamed of
And that dream for me came true.

Now here we are in our golden years
You're still my only one
And when our lives are over here
In eternity, we'll walk as one.

Forever

Can you hear the beating of my heart?

It beats for you.

Can you feel my breath?

I breathe for you.

Can you see the sparkle in my eyes?

It's the reflection of you.

Can you hear my voice?

I love you.

Can you see my smile?

It's because of you.

Can you take my hand in yours?

I am here for you.

Can you feel my touch?

I am always near.

Can you sense my spirit?

We are one.

Can you feel my kiss?

It's forever.

Only You

I wish that I had just one more chance

To hold you close, just one more dance.

To feel your touch, your sweet caress

To feel your breath upon my chest.

I'm dying inside without you here

Even though you're gone I still feel you near.

Just when I think I'm doing fine

It hits me again. God, I can't stop crying.

I miss you more as time goes on

There are only nights, daylight is gone.

So many years we shared together

No I won't get over you, no, not ever.

My heart has been ripped out of my chest

With you, only you, was when I was best.

My days are empty my nights are so cold

It's only with you I wanted to grow old.

I'm lost, just so lost without you by my side

I awake from this dream only to realize I've died.

Fools

You don't know what you've done
Your sick, sadistic game
You've subjected him to such torment
He hangs his head in shame.

You're evil and relentless
You tease and punish him.
He's drowning, you are killing him
How much longer can he swim?

All because he's different
All because you're blind
Is there nothing you won't stop at?
Why are you so unkind?

You take such joy in what you're doing
Because you are a fool
You're a bully and take pleasure
In being hurtful and so cruel.

Eventually you win
And you're so proud of what you've done
Your friends and you, oh such big men!
All against just one.

To escape he took his life
An act of sheer despair.
He cries out from his grave
God why were they so unfair?

But God watches every single person

And all that you have done

Those of you who have caused this

Will be dealt with by the Holy One.

"What if the kid you bullied at school grew up, and turned out to be the only surgeon that could save your life?"

~Lynette Mather

Everything

You're my life, my love, my everything

You're my summer, winter, fall and spring.

You're my sunshine each and every day

You're the blooming flowers in the month of May.

You're the gentle breeze on a butterfly's wings

You're the reason that I want to dance and sing.

You're the northern lights, so magical and bright

You're the moon, the stars, that light up the night.

You're the air I breathe, my heart beats for you

You're the lift I need when I'm feeling blue.

You're everything, such a perfect sweet soul

You're a gift from God, my life is now whole.

Every Step

Do not fear,

It will grip you and not let go.

Do not worry,

Worry changes nothing.

Do not doubt,

Have faith in what you do

Do not be afraid to grieve,

You will heal.

Do not be greedy,

You can't take it with you.

Do not judge,

For you too will be judged.

Do not be cruel,

You reap what you sow.

Do not ridicule,

The joke may be on you.

Do not hate,

It will consume you.

Do not wish someone harm,

You may get what you wish for.

Do not lose faith,

It will carry you through.

Do not doubt God,

He is there every step of the way.

Hands of Time

Here we are

At the fork in two roads.

You have your road

And I have mine.

Somewhere at a point in time

Shall we meet again?

Who knows how many dragons we have slain

Or how many demons we have laid to rest.

When we meet again

Will I still have that thirst for you

Which has been with me forever?

When you see me

Will your eyes peer deep into my soul?

Would their fire reach into my heart,

And warm the coldness that has been there since we parted?

Shall love survive at the hands of time, or will it be erased

Like the dragons and demons we have left behind?

Am I the princess that the prince has come to rescue?

Or fearing we never meet again

Will I wander and search forever?

Neither you nor I hold the answers

So let us be on our way

Wherever we may travel

Through life's journeys, trials, conquests, and hardships, I hope

Fate smiles upon us

And our lives cross paths once again.

Count on Me

You can count on me to be there
Every second of every day.
This deep love that I have for you
Will never fade away.

I'll walk this road of life with you
Even though it may get rough.
I'll be there when you can't go on
When you feel you've had enough.

My heart beats every beat with yours
I'll be there when you're sad.
I'll comfort you and hold you close
When things get really bad.

Your eyes fill up my spirit
Your smile lights up my day.
You speak in words so filled with love
In everything you say.

The years will march on by,
But our love will stay so true.
It's always been there and always will be
This love I have for you.

Comfort

"You must go," God commanded as He heard the cries for help.

The angel descended from the heavens above

And swept up the woman in his arms.

She was weeping and had given up.

The angel held her and whispered "Have faith."

She closed her eyes, so profoundly tired, so lost.

She had no fight left, just emptiness and despair.

"Let me sleep."

Her face was sallow, her eyes welled up with tears.

She had been through so much.

"Don't give up -

Don't give up; have faith!" the angel cried.

She heard his words and felt the love.

Through her tears she saw him

A smile, a love so strong she had never experienced.

Peace, comfort.

"You will go on, you are healed".

"God and all His angels are with you."

The angel lovingly laid her down.

"I am never far." "Sleep now, you are restored," a gentle whisper.

She watched as he ascended into the golden light.

With her spirit renewed, suffering no more

She had been saved.

A Special Place

When you think there is no way out, a door always opens.

When you think there is no chance, you are given another.

When you feel nothing but darkness, the sun shines.

When you come to a dead end, there is a light at the end of the tunnel.

When you get to the highest peak, you will find a valley.

When you are thirsty and weak, the rain will fall.

When you are cold and tired, there is fire and warmth.

When you can't go on, He will carry you.

When you laugh, it lifts your spirit and the spirit of others.

When you cry, your soul will heal and be cleansed.

When you show an act of kindness, He shines His light on you.

When you live a life of cruelty, it will come back to haunt you.

When you show compassion and kindness, it heals.

When you show greed and vanity, it will ruin you.

When you put yourself on a pedestal, you will surely fall.

When you put Him on a pedestal, you will rise.

When you do unto others, you will have it done unto you.

When you forgive, your spirit will be free, and it will soar.

When you live your life serving God, you will live a life of grace and peace.

When you leave this world, He will have a special place for you.

Paradise

There's a place where tails wag freely and treats never end

Where you can romp and jump and play and always have a friend.

This place is filled with chew toys and stuffed animals galore,

And you can go anywhere to dig, to run, to explore.

There are no leashes or kennels, no rules, your senses are keen

It's filled with love and happiness and endless fields of green.

You'll never grow old in this special place, pain free you'll always be

You can do your business anywhere, lift your leg on any tree.

Your fur no longer grey and your nose so black and wet

Your eyes will sparkle like diamonds and you'll never be upset.

The love there will surround you and there you'll be kept safe for me.

Someday I'll come to meet you, until then in heaven you'll be.

So for now I cherish your memory, you're always in my heart

Know when I come to paradise we never again will have to part.

"Dogs are a special blessing. Treat them with love and kindness."

I'm Coming Home

It's a little past midnight, and everything's still except the beating of my heart

It's the same every night, in the dark of our room since we were torn apart.

I close my weary eyes while I hold you close to me

But you are not here; then it all comes back, it's just a tragic memory.

That day was like every other day, you kissed me and said goodbye

In my dreams I feel your gentle caress and see that sparkle in your eyes.

Such peace and comfort knowing that I am with the one I love.

I sigh and smile contentedly and thank the Lord above.

I awake to the dreadful reality, reliving that terrible day.

You called and said "I love you, I'm coming home; I'm on my way."

The shadows grew long through the windows and then darkness filled the room

I sat and waited for you to drive up, hours since you said you'd be home.

Startled by the sound of the doorbell, I thought - silly, he forgot his key.

Smiling to myself with excitement, I opened the door and was shocked to see.

Somber faces stared into mine, two men in uniform.

My eyes welled up, I was ripped away, into the ominous storm.

They informed me you were gone, that you would not be coming home,

In the stillness of the night with my heart ripped out, I stood there all alone.

My life is changed forever, with you no longer here with me

I will live my life as best I can, praying together once again we'll be.

When I close my eyes and drift off to sleep, I feel your presence and your touch.

Your gentle voice whispers to me, "I love you so very much".

Three Years and Twenty-One Days

Dear God it's me, we need to talk, I'm having a really bad day.

It's been three years and twenty-one days since you took my love away.

They said that time would heal the pain that I must carry on

I've really tried, but I'm so filled with grief, I fear that they were wrong.

I tried to pack his clothes away, but I found his favourite tie.

It smelled like him, I broke down again, and all I did was cry.

I eat alone, his place is empty, and I remember the talks we had.

He always knew just what to say to cheer me up when I was sad.

Sometimes I sit in his favourite chair, praying I'll feel him there.

I've searched for him for so long now, but can't find him anywhere.

I miss the way he'd look at me, his eyes so kind and blue.

The gentle way he'd whisper to me, "My darling, I love you."

I miss his smile, I crave his laugh and the feel of my hand in his.

This wasn't supposed to happen to us, our union was wedded bliss.

When I'm asleep he's there with me but when I wake up it's just a dream.

I try to lead a normal life, but I am heartbroken and just want to scream.

My heart feels as though it's about to burst, this ache so deep in my chest.

No one in this world could compare, I had the very best.

I guess I just needed to tell you that I'm having a really bad day.

It's been three years and twenty-one days since you took my love away.

"May there be comfort in knowing that someone so special will never be forgotten."

-Julie Hèbert

Blessed by God

I felt it from the very start

That you and I would never part.

From the moment that you touched my hand

I knew that you would understand.

When I laid my head upon your chest

I knew that I could safely rest.

The way you spoke and held me tight

There was no more darkness, only light.

Your eyes speak of your love for me

With you is where I want to be.

You care for me and are always there

Even when life seems so unfair.

Through the raging storms and the calm thereafter

Will be many years of love and laughter.

You're my best friend and the love of my life,

I was blessed by God to be your wife.

I Miss You

I miss your head upon my lap, the feel of your velvety ears

It's only been a while, but it feels like a thousand years.

I miss your big brown eyes and your muzzle in my hand

The way you'd bring your toys to me, beside me you would stand.

I miss the big old kisses and the way you'd bark and play

I miss you every second of every single day.

I miss the feel of your apricot coat and the velvety black fur on your face

The way your ears fell loosely, so big and out of place.

I miss you lying up on the couch or curled up in my bed

I'm trying so hard to get over this pain, this desperate feeling of dread.

I miss you each and every second, of every single day.

My dear best friend, my precious dog, why did you go away?

"Dogs' lives are too short. Their only fault really."
~ Agnes Sligh Turnbull

My Creator

In the depths of despair

He will carry me.

When I feel I can't go on

He will lift me up.

When my nights are dark

He will give them light.

When fear grips me

He calms me and gently speaks to me.

When worry consumes me

He eases my concerns.

When grief strikes

He heals.

When there is laughter, love and peace

He rejoices.

He's my God, my salvation and my savior.

He's the creator of all, of everything.

"If you lose faith, you lose all."

~ Eleanor Roosevelt

Anna Lachman

Remember the Holocaust

Some say it never happened
They deny that it took place
An evil man's destructive dream
To have his own super race.

With blood on his hands
He made his plans with cruel determination
One by one he took their lives
Doomed to extermination.

In his mind so sick and warped
He murdered and he schemed
His followers were brainwashed
While the innocent begged and screamed.

He took away their home, their pride
Painted a mark upon their chest
And with this mark they carried
They could never hide or rest.

His armies came and herded them
Like cattle to the slaughter
They were crammed into railway cars
No toilets. No food. No water.

Each car held a hundred souls
No room, they were forced to stand
Warned to keep their silence

Walk With Me

Or be dealt a deadly hand.

Promised that they'll not be hurt
Just do as you are told -
So, in silent fear they trusted
What did the future hold?

After many days, their journey's at an end
They finally arrived at their destination
Around the bend in the dark of night
They could see they lights of the railway station.

They wearily climbed from their hideous box
They were gripped with terror and fear
The women and children were separated
From the men that they held dear.

They shuffled slowly towards the camp
Watched their men go to the right
It was the last time that they saw them
As loved ones faded into the night.

The ominous chimney it towered so high
What was this foreign place?
How could they know it was the end
What they were about to face?

The ones who were spared from a fiery hell
Were put in blocks to live
Terror filled their hollow eyes, exhausted
They had nothing left to give.

The henchmen were cruel, the beatings many

Anna Lachman

The conditions were most grave
Only bread and broth were given
To ration, to share, to save.

Forced to work countless hours
They got very little rest.
To stay alive each must be strong
For life itself was a daily quest.

The months went by, the suffering grew
Each and every body became a sunken shell.
Beatings, starvation, and torture
Were endured in this living hell.

Train after train carried human cargo
To the land of the living dead.
Thousands of innocent victims,
In their eyes the same look of dread.

Mountains of bodies piled high
Where thousands had met their end
The stench wafted through the air
A message of death it would send.

And all the while they perished
This evil man was not satisfied
His armies grew, he sent them out
"Not enough of them have died!"

So on it went and he rejoiced
In the butchering, horror and pain
Concentration camps stocked with souls
Death to them all was his ruthless claim

But then one day, the allies came

The fortunate ones had gained freedom back

For some it was a joyous day

But for many a day of black.

To a bunker deep in the woods

This monster had fled and run.

Like the coward he was, he took his life

To his head he raised a gun.

For those who made it to the end

That survived this living hell

They were broken, never the same again

Even though the enemy fell.

Their families gone, now all alone

Where would they go from here?

Some went mad, others became silent

But most common, there was fear.

The memories of their living hell

And of loved ones they had lost

How could they ever forget

They had lived through the Holocaust?

"To forget a Holocaust is to kill twice."
~Elie Wiesel

Because You Left

My heart doesn't know why you left

It's still beating

Still pumping

Still breaking.

My mind can't comprehend

Understand

Reason or fathom

Why this happened.

My spirit is broken

Weeping

Searching and screaming

Lost in the abyss.

My body is aching

Yearning

Wanting to feel you

But you aren't here.

My soul is lost without its soulmate

Torn apart

Lonely

Bereaved and forlorn.

It shines no more

Because you left.

Why Are We Here?

Why walk when you can run?

Why cry when you can laugh?

Why turn away when you can help?

Why help if you want something in return?

Why stay angry when you can forgive?

Why forgive if you don't mean it?

Why be jealous when you have all you need?

Why be envious when you are given it all?

Why turn the other way when someone needs help?

Why not walk in another man's shoes?

Why do you see only in black and white?

Why can't you see the colours of the world?

Why look for something that is not lost?

Why not see that it is right there in front of you?

Why take a foolish chance that could end your life?

Why not live your life wisely until the end?

Why not live to the fullest every day?

Why worry about tomorrow or dwell on yesterday?

Why be fearful when He is there every step of the way?

Why not live, love, laugh, forgive, run, sing and dance?

Why are we here?

To make a difference in this world.

Carry Me

Is there somewhere I can hide from these emotions

That have ripped me away from reality?

I am filled with the unsurmountable pain and suffering

That worry has caused me.

Worry doesn't change a thing, yet here I am

Caught in a catastrophic storm of fear

The fear of not knowing

Yes, of not knowing.

And, with that, how do I continue to live and enjoy life?

How can I rest peacefully

Knowing that the fear and worry will torment me

Hunt me down, no matter where I am

It will stalk me and finally consume me.

"Oh Father, please do not forsake me.

I am weary.

Lift me up and give me strength.

For if you don't I will surely crumble and cease to be."

I gaze upwards then bow my head in prayer,

The pain flows through my tears

As they fall on my clenched hands.

"I beg you for strength, hope and peace.

Surround me with your guardians so that I don't stand alone

And I will surrender to you my body and soul.

My spirit will soar for you did not desert me.

You are my God.

Carry me now."

"No matter what storm you face, you need to know that God loves you. He has not abandoned you."

~ Franklin Graham

Anna Lachman

How Dare You?

You snuck up on me quietly, rudely.

This is my body but you violated it

Without a sign, no notice,

A thief in the night.

How dare you?

So many of us you have invaded

As we go about our daily lives

As you silently grow inside of us

We think everything is fine.

We feel fine and then we are given the news.

How dare you?

Do you know how I felt when I found out about you?

My world crashed down all around me.

I lay in bed for days and sobbed.

I was mentally defeated.

I was terrified.

How dare you?

Once so strong, vivacious, so full of life

You have weakened me.

I am praying for strength as I must fight you.

How dare you?

I am well into my treatments

I am battling you with everything I have.

I am praying to the Lord that you will not win

I "will" you to be gone

Walk With Me

How dare you!

So many, you have robbed them of life,

From their loved ones,

From their hopes and dreams.

My world has been turned upside down

Because of you.

How dare you?

I will not let you beat me

You will not win!

I have the Lord and all His angels

Here with me to battle you.

I will fight.

I will live.

I will be victorious.

I will not let cancer take me.

"The human spirit is stronger than anything that can happen to it."

~C.C. Scott

Easy

Live your life by doing what's right

Steering clear of what's wrong

And following the laws of the Lord.

Don't expect anything in return for an act of kindness

It should just come natural

Out of the goodness of your heart.

It should not be done in return for something.

God is watching your every move

And is with you every step of the way.

Through all the trials you will go through in your life

He is with you.

All the suffering and hardships

He is with you.

All the love and kindness He sees

And with that you will be rewarded by Him!

Don't give if you expect something in return.

Don't be cruel

You will answer for it.

At the end of your time on earth

God the King will be standing there.

He will open the gates of heaven and you will be welcome.

This will be your reward

And all because you showed kindness and were good.

Should be easy.

"Kindness is free to give, but priceless to receive."

My Soulmate

I need to have you near me
Feel your warmth and gentle touch
Oh, darling, how I love you
I love you oh so much.

When you hold me in your arms,
And softly speak to me
I know I've found my soulmate
God has meant for us to be.

I remember when I met you
The way I felt inside
My love for you was instant
I just know it will never die.

I think of you when we're apart,
And I am half without you there
I can't believe I searched so long
I looked for you everywhere.

So hold me tight against your chest
Let our hearts beat together as one
Together we will always be
Until our time on earth is done.

And when I take my very last breath
I hope that you will know
That I will love you forever
A love that will only grow.

Anna Lachman

For what is true here on earth

Two people bound by love

Will carry on forever

In the heavens up above.

"There is no accidental meetings between souls."

~ Sheila Burke

How Could You?

I was young, a teenage boy

Full of enthusiasm

Excited about my future.

Even though you teased me relentlessly

I still had hope.

How could you?

I was small for my age

A late bloomer

Kind and gentle by nature

Just a kid from the farm.

Shy and quiet

I tried so hard to fit in.

I was smart, I got good grades

I needed my glasses to read

And you stole them.

My parents couldn't afford new ones,

I struggled without them.

My grades started to suffer.

How could you?

My parents couldn't afford to buy me a car

Like so many of you had.

I walked to school or rode my bike.

You followed me

Narrowly missing me with your fancy cars.

You stalked me, I was so afraid.

How could you?

Some of the girls felt sorry for me,

But some of them actually liked me

For the person I was.

For some reason you felt threatened by this

It made you angry.

How could you?

You would play horrible tricks on me

Oh, you were so cruel.

You would chase me and catch me

You would lock me in the lockers in the boys change room.

I waited for hours to be set free, barely able to breathe

Alone in the dark.

I was petrified to confide to the principal

For fear of retribution

I suffered quietly.

How could you?

You tore up my books

You stole my journal and read it out loud

I was mortified.

You stole my lunch and I went without.

You followed me into the boys washroom

I had no privacy.

You called me a geek, loser, a wimp.

Humiliated and embarrassed I suffered in silence.

How could you?

You beat me up because you thought it was funny

You destroyed my bike, my only transportation.

It amused you.

You felt superior and tough.

Walk With Me

Oh yes, you were so cool!

You laughed while I was dying inside.

How could you?

You wondered where I was when I didn't show up

For school that day.

Who would you pick on now?

Did you feel any guilt at all

When you heard I'd taken my life?

You broke my spirit.

My life was cut short because of you

My soul cries out in agony and pain.

How could you?

"Blowing out someone else's candle doesn't make yours shine any brighter."

Anna Lachman

Even the Small

I found you in the cold one day
Small and frail, so lost.
I tried so hard to save you
I'd do anything at any cost.

Oh baby mouse, so tiny and lost
How will you possibly survive?
I know it sounds impossible
But I will try to keep you alive.

I kept him warm and prayed for him
That God would let him live.
Too small to live without his mom
I knew this I couldn't give.

The hours passed by and I could see
That his little spirit was growing weak.
I picked him up and said a prayer
And held him to my cheek.

He took a breath and let out a sigh
I knew the end was near.
I cradled him in my hands, to keep him warm
In a moment, he wasn't there.

I know it was just a little mouse
To many, nothing at all.
But God created everything
Even the very small.

I found a place to lay him to rest

And buried him in that spot.

Under my favourite rose bush is where he lies

He will never be forgot.

"When man learns to respect even the smallest being of creation...nobody has to teach him to love his fellow man."

~ Albert Schweitzer

Anna Lachman

Don't Drink and Drive

I always listened to what you said

"Be safe, don't drink and drive,"

You warned me of the dangers

"Be safe to stay alive."

Many nights you'd lie awake,

And wait for me to come home.

Your worries and your fears, dear Mom,

You'd wait there all alone.

You didn't have to worry so

I remember all you taught

"Be safe, don't drink and drive."

Those words I never forgot.

My friends would tease and say

"Come on, oh, it will be alright."

But I always kept my common sense

Remembering wrong from right.

Now here I lay, darkness all around.

Flashing lights and sirens scream

Oh God, what is happening? What went wrong?

This must be a horrible dream.

I know you're lying at home in bed

Waiting for the sound of my car

Please know, dear Mom

I almost made it home, I wasn't very far.

I was safe and didn't drink and drive

Just went to visit a friend

I didn't see it coming Mom,

As he sped around the bend.

Walk With Me

The blinding lights came into my lane,

And his car tore into mine.

I tried to get out of his way, but Mom

I didn't have time.

He was drunk, he shouldn't have driven,

And yet he made that choice.

I can feel you reaching out to me

I can hear your soothing voice.

Now here I lie, on this summer's night

I see my blood all around.

Cold and scared I think of you

As I lie here on the ground.

There are people all around me now

They're trying to save my life

It hurts, oh God, as they move me Mom,

It's cutting like a knife.

It's time for me to go now Mom

My life is slipping away.

I feel a warmth and there's a glowing light

I guess I'm on my way.

I feel at peace, the pain is gone Mom,

I'm going into the light.

I love you so, please carry on

And for me, carry on the fight.

If everyone would listen

Don't be foolish, don't drink and drive

Just think how many lives we'd save;

Maybe I would still be alive.

"Dedicated to MADD"

Anna Lachman

One of a Kind

Your life is very special

You are one of a kind

Don't doubt it for a moment

Another you won't find.

Every single human being

Was created from up above

The Lord made you to be here

He created you with love.

The animals and foliage

Were made to share this earth

We all are here for a purpose

Assigned to us at birth.

Treat all with love and gentleness

Be kind and you will see

Our world will be a better place

For all humanity.

A Grandparent's Prayer

Puff the magic dragon; twinkle, twinkle little star

Close your eyes and make a wish, for I am never far.

Peter, Peter pumpkin-eater; cock-a-doodle-doo

My precious little grandchildren, I'll always be here for you.

This little piggy; tweedle-dum and tweedle-dee

You are my angels from up above - God protect thee.

Rub-a-dub-dub; the three blind mice

You're always safe with me, never think twice.

Mary had a little lamb; and remember Old King Cole

Bless your shining spirits and your precious souls.

"Dedicated to my grandson Trysten and granddaughter Kayden Hope"

Anna Lachman

In Search of You

I've searched by night, I've searched by day

I can't understand why you went away.

I've searched for you in the morning sun

I've looked for you in every one.

I've stared upon the moon, and still

There's that empty spot only you can fill.

I've wished upon a falling star

My wish is that you weren't so far.

I've stood out in the pouring rain

In hopes that maybe I'd see you again.

I've stared out at the roaring sea

Praying that you'd come back to me.

I've felt the wind upon my face

You left me all alone in this place.

I've walked alone for so long now

Oh please come back, just tell me how.

I've spent my days in search of you

Is this what broken hearted lovers do?

Peace on Earth

Protect and love one another.

Embrace the beauty of this world.

Allow yourself quiet moments of reflection.

Cruelty is a sin; be kind and compassionate.

Endeavor to be the best you can be.

Overlook the small things, they are trivial.

Nobody is perfect, we are all individuals.

End grudges and bad feelings towards others.

Accept the things you cannot change.

Respect yourself and others, help those in need.

Trust your instincts and listen to your heart.

Have faith, persevere, and follow your dreams.

Anna Lachman

My Treasure

Like a beautiful flower on a dew-kissed morn

You were sent straight from heaven the day you were born.

The sun shined so bright and the birds danced with joy

The heavens rejoiced, God has sent us a boy.

Ten little fingers and ten little toes

The face of an angel, your spirit just glows.

My life's changed forever, my heart's filled with love

This precious little boy, my treasure from above.

"For Trysten - I love you bigger than life."

A Second Chance

They hear you beyond the door
This could be the day.
Some growl and bark, others cry and whimper,
Some just want to play.

Here they live with concrete floors
And iron bars all around.
Some were abused and neglected
Some abandoned and then found.

Old and young, every shape and size
Desperate they sit and wait
For someone to give them a loving home
For someone to open the gate.

Their eyes they plead don't leave me here
Don't leave me here all alone.
I'm lonely and I'm so afraid
Please can you take me home?

A second chance is all they ask
Free from the long lonely days.
They just want your love
If given a chance they're sure to win your praise.

There isn't much time,
Many are put to sleep, while waiting to be freed.
Man's best friend, it's just not fair
Their sad eyes look at you and plead.

93

So go to a shelter, open the door,

And give just one a loving home.

Many can be saved, just open your heart

Don't leave them there all alone.

"Rescue does not mean damaged, it means let down by humans."

It's Not a Dream

I woke up in a different place
A dream, or was it real?
Confused but very peaceful
A strange way to feel.

I noticed all my pain was gone
My worries and my fears
My body felt so much stronger
Hadn't felt this good in years.

How strange it felt to move with ease
This had to be a dream
I felt the sun above me, birds singing
Heard a bubbling stream.

With mounting joy and a bounce in my step
I headed for the door
It's not a dream, it opened to heaven
Eternal peace, suffering no more.

"For Patti. Rest easy my dear friend."

Listen

Oh Lord, my heart is heavy
Just look what man has done.
How many chances you've given us
He died for us, your Son.

You've blessed us with forgiveness
A second chance and grace
You created us in your image
The entire human race.

The heavens must be filled
With angels weeping at the sight
Of man's evil and corruption
His destruction and his plight.

I pray for all the people
From every corner of the earth
Fall to your knees, raise up your hands
And pray for man's rebirth.

Ask God for His forgiveness
Be kind, "Thou shalt not kill."
The angels want to help
Close your eyes, listen, be still.

We all must love one another
We are all God's children you see
For to unburden His heart, free your spirit and soul
Love and peace, faith and harmony, must be.

"Peace is the only battle worth waging."

~Albert Camus

Anna Lachman

Our Spirits Live Forever

The Whitemud Creek, the Blackmud Creek, the North Saskatchewan,

The prairie plains are silenced now, no more buffalo run.

They came and took our land, why can't we live in peace?

This hatred and this greed, when will it ever cease?

God made enough for everyone, but still they wanted more

So, with freedom in our hearts we fought a bloody war.

They've taken many lives, proud of what they've done

But our spirits live forever by the North Saskatchewan.

Yes our spirits live forever, no match for any gun.

Until we Meet Again

Today began like every other day

The sun shined so bright as people crossed the bay.

The skies were clear on this September morn

People rushed to work, babies were born.

A horrifying destruction of innocent precious lives

Husbands, fathers, sons, mothers, daughters, sisters, wives.

It happened without warning, gone forever are the towers

The work of evil people, the devil and his followers.

The Trade Centre was destroyed, the Pentagon was hit too

A field in Pennsylvania, the skies no longer blue.

Many thousands senselessly died, a horrifying, cowardly act

Dear God, we're terrified and angry, how are we to react?

Oh Father, heal our grief, our hatred and our pain

We pray for those in heaven, keep them safe until we meet again.

"In memory of all of those who perished on 9/11/01."

Anna Lachman

We Never Said Goodbye

It's been a while since I heard your voice, I thought of you today

Memories of you filled my thoughts as I went about my day.

I reminisce of years gone by when youth was on our side

Your laughter and your beauty, your energy and pride.

I dreamt of you again dear friend, I need to talk to you

So many things I should have said, you never really knew.

You need to know I love you, and you're always in my heart

It's hard for me to accept that we were forced apart.

Today I thought I heard your voice, dear friend, I miss you so

The angels came and took you, it was time for you to go.

I felt you tug at my soul, my spirit heard your cry

I never got to talk to you, we never said goodbye.

"In loving memory of Linda."

"Many people will walk in and out of your life, but only true friends will leave footprints in your heart."

~Eleanor Roosevelt

Young Man

"Can you help me?" "Yes I can."

"Can you heal me?" He raised His hands.

"Please forgive me," the young man said

"Please don't deny me." He bowed his head.

"Can you give me strength and love,

And faith in the power from Heaven above?"

With that He raised His hands up high

The young man prayed as He parted the sky.

"Don't be afraid," the young man was told

As the sky opened up the earth shimmered like gold.

Then God touched his heart, blessed his body and soul

Forgiven and healed, once again he was whole.

"Please don't despair, keep your faith, don't be blue,"

Young man when in need, by your side I'll be true."

"God loves each of us as if there was only one of us"

~Augustine

A Smile

A smile can brighten the darkest of days

Kind words can help chase all your worries away.

A hug can uplift and show that you care

Good friends are a treasure to find them is rare.

A song can warm hearts, bring peace and good cheer

It heals and inspires, it's a release from your fears.

A prayer can change lives, bring you faith, hope and love

God smiles down upon you from heaven above.

"A Smile is the beauty of the soul."
~Lailah Gifty Akita

A Thousand Tears

Here's a piece of my heart, it's broken anyway

I'll pick up the pieces, now carry on, leave, be on your way.

Here's what's left of my mind, I thought I really knew you

A thousand tears I'd given, the happy times so few.

Here's my eyes, take one last look, no longer brown but blue

But they will heal, the tears will dry, as memories fade of you.

Here's my arms I held you in, you'll never feel again

In time they'll hold another, where am I you'll wonder then

Here's my ring, your broken vows, the bond of love has died.

I'll carry on, my heart will heal, I have Jesus by my side.

Angels Amongst Us

Angels walk amongst us every day, right here on earth

We're all assigned a guardian from the moment of our birth.

God knows we're only human and will need help along the way

So He's given us His messengers to be with us every day.

They're here to guide, protect and love - to bring you peace and joy

From all the corners of the world, every girl and every boy.

So when you need your angels help, in an instant they'll be there

Fall to your knees, raise up your hands and fill the heavens with prayer.

For every moment you lose a little hope, your angels whisper, "Don't worry, I am with you."

Farewell to Summer

The leaves are turning golden orange, the air is cool and crisp

The days much shorter now and nights are long, with winter on the horizon.

I heard the geese announce their departure as they formed a familiar shape

As they flew so high up above and headed for warmer days.

The musky scent of the harvest as the crops are put to rest, and the northern winds

Are sending the message of the frost that will soon start the freeze.

The buffalo and the elk, all animals of every size

Are sensing another summer has passed,

And will rest and keep warm as they huddle together.

The trees are almost naked as the crisp winds loosen their leaves

And blow them around in a whirlwind dance of crimson and gold

To finally rest and wait for the snow.

The fragrance of fireplaces burning sweet-smelling birch

Thanksgiving is upon us again

How we love family and friends, apple cider and pumpkin pie.

As we bid farewell to summer, give thanks for the chance

To have enjoyed and loved

To behold the beauty of all that God has given us.

Gone

Across the room I noticed him for a moment, then gone

Then gone was I, my mind somewhere else, sadness,

Sadness and heartache, a tear, remembering,

Remembering my love now gone, his face,

His face etched in my mind, his warm smile,

His warm smile and kind eyes, his gentle touch

Oh God, his sweet voice, his warmth,

Warm me no more. Where has he gone?

Gone with God, he's gone home,

Home to heaven, just across the room.

"A piece of my heart lives in Heaven"

Goodbye

It's not what you say, it's what you don't.

It's not how you look, it's that you won't.

It's not in your touch, you don't feel.

It's not in your eyes, they're like steel.

It's not in your heart, it is cold.

It's not in your mind, you're too bold.

It's not in your body or soul

It's my spirit that's taken the toll.

It's not what I dreamed it should be

It's the end of us, you can't see.

It's a choice that I make, it's goodbye.

If I stay my spirit will die.

It's a choice I must make.

It's goodbye.

I Needed to Pray

I went for a walk on a late summer day

I went for a walk, I needed to pray.

I prayed to my Father as I walked through the trees

I laughed with my angels as they played in the leaves.

I went for a walk to give thanks for the day

I went for a walk, I wanted to pray.

I rejoiced in the glory of today's rising sun

I rejoiced in it's setting, I thanked God for every one.

I can't help but notice the birds are so few

They'll be back in the spring, another year new.

I went for a walk, I felt God touch my soul

Down my favourite path, this is where I feel whole.

The scent of the harvest, the crispness in the air,

To know that my Father will always be there.

I went for a walk on a late autumn day

I went for a walk, I needed to pray.

"He who kneels the most, stands the best."

~D.L. Moody

My Love for You

My heart aches for your touch, my eyes cannot see

My lips do not smile, I hear nothing, I'm not free.

My arms long for the feel of you here by my side

My body and soul have since seemingly died.

My senses have left me, I'm withered and torn

Like a rose without water, I'm lost and forlorn.

My days have no sunlight, my nights filled with pain

I dream of the time when we're together again.

This longing for you will always be here

The memories of us I will forever hold dear.

I will patiently wait, if it takes the rest of my life

We were meant to be together as husband and wife.

"True love stories never have endings."

~Richard Bach

Life's Little Things

Enjoy the little things in your life, smell the roses along the way
Small things are important, they help us through the day.
Life is filled with worries, hardships, sometimes fear
Remember, it's the little things that bring you through the year.
A child's laugh, a father's hug, a mother's soothing touch,
To hear your loved one tell you "I love you very much."
A candy cane, an ice cream cone, fresh baked bread and apple pie,
Snowy days, autumn leaves, spring showers and July.
A brand new puppy, a kitten's purr, the softness of a dove
All animals are sent to us, a gift from God above.
So when you're feeling tired, afraid, or even blue
Remember, enjoy life's little things, they'll help to see you through.

A Difference

I want to make a difference in the world

An impact on people's lives.

We all must love one another

Brothers, sisters, fathers, mothers, husbands and wives.

I want to live my entire life serving God

And doing what's right

To lend an ear, a helping hand

To have a clear conscience at night.

I want to smell the rain so sweet,

And behold the rising sun

Appreciate the glory of each new day,

And thank God for every one.

I want to give of myself

To love and help those in need

From every corner of the earth

Religion, colour, or creed.

I want to serve my Lord above

So when my time has come

The gates of heaven will open up,

And the angels will take me home.

"If you change the way you look at things the things you look at change."
~Wayne Dyer

We Agree

We agree, we always would say

It kept us strong every day.

We agree, awake and in sleep

To Him we'd pray for us to keep.

We agree to be strong, good health

For all of us bring peace and wealth.

We agree, in the darkest of hours

God is there with all His powers.

We agree, in work and in play

Protect us Lord, every day.

We agree as long as there's two

Our bond in life will carry us through.

We agree for all eternity

To be together, you and me.

"To My Precious Mom"

Memory Lane

Take a trip down memory lane but try not to stay there long.

It's good to have old memories but don't dwell on what's gone wrong.

Life's too short so live for today,

At any time we could be called away.

Live each day in harmony

Rewards are great - you will see.

Do unto others as you'd have done

Laugh and hug, play and have fun.

Love your parents with all of your soul.

Children make your spirit whole.

Behold each day, it's beauty and grace

God has given us such a beautiful place.

Be honest and kind, thou shalt not steal -

Remember the commandments, they are real.

Do not kill, life is not yours to take

One of God's rules you must not forsake.

A smile, a hug, a reassuring word

To hear "I love you" when it's never been heard.

Visit the past but come back to today

Tomorrow is waiting, don't forget to pray.

"We have to pray with our eyes on God, not on the difficulties."
~Oswald Chambers

Let Go

Let go of your fear, your anger and pain

Ask God to come into your heart once again.

Open your eyes, your spirit and soul

For to pray to your Father will again make you whole.

No matter how frightened and beaten you feel

The power of prayer - it's the answer, it's real.

Have faith in His angels, the power above

God sends you these guardians with His message of love.

They're here to protect you, to guide you and heal

Some say in their presence God's love you can feel.

From the sun to the stars and the oceans so blue

Across every land, believe in Him - His love is true.

Sully

They say a dog is man's best friend

And this you were, right to the end.

Your gentle soul and spirit so true

In you, dear friend, I have such love for you.

From the moment you were born, from the very first touch

My heart was filled with joy, I loved you so much.

A gentle giant, with soft ears and brown eyes

I search for you now in God's heavenly skies.

You made my life such a beautiful place

My memories of you will never be erased.

You are etched in my heart, God I miss you so much

I wish you were here to hold and to touch.

When my earth time is done, watch for me on the ridge

I'll come join you at the rainbow bridge.

What a glorious reunion that will be

Together, forever, in eternity.

"In Loving memory of Sully, my precious friend and canine companion."

I Wish

I thought of you today and wondered how you were.

Were you someplace warm, with the wind caressing your face?

Oh, how I wish I were the wind.

Were you happy, laughing that contagious laugh

That made everyone smile and feel good inside?

Oh, how I wish I could hear you.

Were your eyes full of life and sparkling blue?

Oh, how I wish I could see you.

Were you in a garden full of your favourite roses

Fragrant and peaceful?

Oh, how I wish I were beside you.

Were you waiting for me to join you

Holding out your hand?

Oh, how I wish you were here.

Were you safe on the other side

In heaven in God's loving care?

Oh how I wish you didn't have to go…

"How lucky I am to have something that makes saying goodbye so hard."

~Winnie The Poo

She

She never had an easy life

From the moment she was born

She lived in fear and poverty

Her clothes were ragged and torn.

Her mother couldn't speak English

And the bottle was her dad's best friend

She was brave and always smiled

Even when her parent's marriage came to an end.

Her mother worked as a cook

For the railways and their men

At the end of a hot and dusty week

The dollars she earned was ten.

She spent most days, aside from school

Busy helping out

She dreamed of a brighter future

As her chores she went about.

She grew into a dark-haired beauty

Her smile was so sweet and kind

And one day on a blind date

She met the man she prayed she'd find.

She was married in her sixteenth year

A clear, warm February day

Oh, she loved this handsome man

He stole her heart away.

She had four sons, a daughter too

Her family was her life.

She smiled when she looked at her kids

She loved being a mother and wife.

Anna Lachman

The years went by so quickly

The children all left home

At least she had her husband

She was comforted that she was not alone.

She never could have imagined

That her love of so many years

Soon would leave her broken

To cry a thousand tears.

She's been through the hardest of times

But with God's loving grace

She will carry on just like she's done

With a smile upon her face.

For my mom…
"God could not be everywhere, and therefore he created mothers."
~Rudyard Kipling

Reach Out

Think for a moment before you speak.

Consider the feelings of those around you.

Don't judge for there is a far greater judge than you.

Walk with your head up high, but not so high that you lose sight.

Arrogance is conceit in disguise, it leaves little room for others.

Reach out your hand, be kind; it may change someone's life.

The rewards will be great, no act of kindness goes unnoticed.

Smile instead of frowning, it will cause a chain reaction of happiness.

Hold others in the palm of your hand, and God will hold you in His.

Family

Forever and always, bonded by love

A gift so very special from Him above

Memories, laughter, hearts held so dear

In knowing the closeness is always right here

Living this life with you all by my side

You've blessed all my days - what a beautiful ride.

"Family is not an important thing, it's everything!"

~ Michael J. Fox

Eternity

I've loved you forever, since the beginning of time

Each step we take is a journey and an adventure.

Every heartbeat is for you.

Every breath I take is with you.

When I sleep I take you with me in my dreams,

And when I awake, the sun shines down upon us.

On the wings of a butterfly we soar together.

Through the seasons we walk hand in hand.

With my head on your chest I feel your love.

Peace and comfort warm my body, soul and spirit.

Together we are on this journey called life.

Our love will carry us through any battle.

When the nights are dark I need not search

For you are beside me, with me, and there is light.

For eternity we are one.

May God hold you close forever.

It Wasn't So Bad

The days leading up to today have been long, difficult and sad,

But with you here right beside me, it really hasn't been so bad.

I look back upon my journey, there were times I cried out in pain,

I know you were there listening and my words weren't all in vain.

My faith at times had faltered, I felt I couldn't go on,

But again I felt you there with me, and I heard your joyous song.

I screamed in pain and anger, my eyes filled with sadness and tears,

I tried so hard to fight this war, please forgive me for all my fears.

I've never walked this road before; God, I gave it all I had,

Thank you for carrying me, Father, because of you it wasn't so bad.

"God will carry you through the storm."

~ Isaiah 43.2

Blessed

Sunshine on my shoulders, the wind upon my face

I'm so blessed to be alive here in this beautiful place.

The morning in its glory, the chickadees chatter and play

The smell of dew-kissed sweet peas, the fresh cut fragrant hay.

The pond in my backyard as the beaver slaps his tail,

He scares away the mallard ducks as he leaves a rippling trail.

The busy little bumblebees where do they get their power?

In a constant search for pollen they dart from flower to flower.

The thorny little porcupine so shy up in the trees,

He slumbers slowly up and down, as he nibbles on the leaves.

The whitetail deer and the buffalo in pastures lush and green,

So peaceful and so beautiful, a truly awesome scene.

The nervous little squirrels, they quarrel as they gather food,

It's their private tribal war, their own little family feud.

The sunset brings a quiet hush except for the neighborly owl,

In the distance you can hear the coyotes, out on their nightly prowl.

The stars and moon and northern lights, they decorate the sky,

And bats awaken from their sleep, these creatures small and shy.

I wouldn't trade the country life, it's the best place I could be,

It's heaven on earth, it's paradise, I am blessed to be so free.

"The love for all living creatures is the most notable attribute of man."

~ Charles Darwin

Anna Lachman

To Eternity

Hold me in your arms, and never let me go,

Kiss me and tell me, I'm the only one you know.

Take my hand in yours, and forever hold it tight,

Through the dark, I'm safe with you, into the morning light.

Walk with me through the seasons of life,

Together as one, as husband and wife.

Run your fingers so lovingly through my hair,

Let me feel you around me everywhere.

Smile that smile that makes everything alright,

Let the passion we share soar and take flight.

To be by your side is the only place for me,

You're the love of my life, today to eternity.

This Dream Come True

I lay here beside you and feel your warmth

And listen to you breathe,

And pray to God from the depths of my soul

That you will never leave.

I feel the beat of your heart

As I place my head upon your chest.

I hold you close to me

And embrace this moment of blissful rest.

In the silence of the night I hear nothing,

Feel nothing but you.

My life is complete, and without you

I would not know what to do.

Your love has been unconditional,

Your spirit shines so bright.

With you in my life there's no darkness,

Just everlasting light.

With you by my side I am strong,

And feel I can conquer it all.

And I know you will always be there,

To catch me when I fall.

Now I lay here silently praying,

With you here next to me.

Anna Lachman

That this dream come true I'm living,

Will forever and always be.

The Girl of My Dreams

So many faces, so shallow so cold

If I search for love here I shall surely grow old.

A sigh and a smile, it's time that I go

Why I'm here in the first place I'll never know.

Then there in the corner, two beautiful warm eyes

Sparkling and sincere, only truth there's no lies.

Her beauty's overwhelming with a sultry feline grace,

But I can't for the life of me approach her sacred space.

Now I sit here in wonder, a miracle it seems

For the Lord has allowed me the girl of my dreams.

Tender love and friendship, all my prayers have come true,

I hold her in my arms whispering softly, "I love you."

To the Heavens I pray that our love will last forever

I'm in awe because I've found such a beautiful treasure.

I am blessed by her presence, my heart beats with pride

The girl of my dreams finally here by my side.

"You were my favorite hello...and my hardest goodbye."

Don't

Don't assume that you are the only one who is having a bad day.

Don't take your anger out on others.

Don't take things too personally.

Don't expect a smile when all you give is a frown.

Don't cry too long over things you cannot change.

Don't turn the other cheek when you have the power to make a difference.

Don't hold grudges, just let it go.

Don't be afraid to stand up for what you believe in.

Don't follow the crowd just to be popular

Don't be afraid to be a leader.

Don't be a leader filled with hate.

Don't make a promise you can't keep.

Don't be so vain that you think you know everything.

Don't miss all the chances you have to learn.

Don't pass by those that are in need.

Don't bully, threaten or ridicule others.

Don't be afraid to hug and comfort those around you.

Don't take life for granted.

Don't assume you can save it for another day.

Don't be afraid to explore life and its beauty.

Don't be foolish and take risks that will end it.

Don't stay down if you fall.

Don't sit if you can stand.

Don't forget to hug your children.

Don't rush the young to grow up so fast.

Don't give up when your world is upside down.

Don't go to sleep mad.

Don't get up angry.

Don't be afraid to grieve.

Walk With Me

Don't think that crying is weak.

Don't hold in a good laugh.

Don't think you're too old to try something new.

Don't worry, you are not alone.

Don't ignore the lonely.

Don't be too hard on yourself if you fail.

Don't be afraid to try again.

Don't worry if you make a mistake.

Don't make mistakes without learning from them.

Don't be too proud to ask for help.

Don't walk away if you can help.

Don't forget to say I'm sorry.

Don't forget to say I love you.

Don't assume they know.

Don't apologize if you don't mean it.

Don't think a broken heart won't mend.

Don't fix something that isn't broken.

Don't miss a sunrise.

Don't miss a sunset.

Don't forget to look at the stars.

Don't miss the chance to go for a walk in the rain.

Don't be cruel to animals.

Don't take them for granted.

Don't mistreat our planet.

Don't forget who put us here.

Don't forget there's a higher power.

Don't believe He's forgotten about you.

Don't forget who your creator is.

Don't lose faith, you're in His loving hands.

The Storm

The canola fields are blazing yellow

With the smell of fresh cut hay in the air

July is here in Alberta, there is beauty and wonder everywhere.

The days are hot and long, then the clouds begin to form,

In the distance you can hear the thunder

And see the approaching storm.

It's always calm before the storm,

And then the wind grabs hold.

The grasses sway and the trees stand strong

And then it starts to unfold.

The lightning lights up the rolling clouds,

And the thunder rumbles again.

And then the earth is covered with the renewing, refreshing rain.

Then all of a sudden it stops,

Like someone's turned off a tap.

The storm has passed and from under the clouds,

Appears the glorious sun.

A rainbow so bright and beautiful forms

A sign the storm is done.

Hoover

I don't know where to go from here
I just don't know where to run.
You left me seven days ago
You were my light and you were my sun.

Your illness, oh you fought so hard
I sensed it wouldn't be long.
I thought I had prepared myself
But I see now I was wrong.

Through it all you never lost
Your dignity or grace.
With a wagging tail you'd come to me
And gently lick my face.

You'd lay with me, and I with you
Soft breaths upon my chest.
Warm brown eyes, and velvet ears
Together we would rest.

I miss the sound of your paws
As you came bounding through the door.
It's silent now, I listen
But can't hear them anymore.

Your silly ways, oh how I laughed
A champion and a clown.
As long as you were here with me
How could I ever be down?

Anna Lachman

God must have a special place

After all you are man's best friend.

A better companion I'll never find

This is not the end.

Watch for me at the rainbow bridge,

For when my days are done,

It's you I will be looking for

My light, my love, my sun.

"In Memory of Hoover. Forever in my heart, always loved."

Floundering

There's still so much I want to say

Since you suddenly left that summer day.

We had so much to talk about

Now I'm left with questions and so much doubt.

Doubt I'll never know more about you

Questions, I still had more than a few.

So many questions, now unanswered remain

I'm desperately trying to find you again.

The reality is you're no longer here

I look to the skies, so blue and clear.

Are you happy and safe up in heaven above?

Are you free of pain and surrounded by love?

Can you see me and sense my broken heart?

I never thought the day would come where we'd have to part.

Now every day is so empty and long

You are what kept me going and strong.

Without you I'm floundering, I'm filled with despair

How I wish I would see you standing there.

Hand outstretched with your smile so warm

We would walk and reminisce, arm in arm.

There isn't a day I don't grieve for you

My heart hurts so bad, I don't know what to do.

Some days I just want to pick up the phone

Then it hits me, you're no longer at home.

From the day I was born, all my life you were there

Now I'm so alone, you aren't anywhere.

It doesn't get easier, the seasons grow longer

Anna Lachman

You were my best friend, my teacher, my precious father.

"You will always be in my heart...because in there you're still alive."
~ Jamie Cirello

Changes

Nothing in the world really changes when a loved one passes away

The sun still rises and sets just like any other day.

Birds still sing, the wind still blows and the rain still falls from above

Babies are born, children still play, lovers still fall in love.

The earth still turns, tides still rise, waves still touch the shore

Winter, spring, summer and fall come and go like they did before

People still go on with their days busy and full of life

The vows of marriage still taken, I pronounce you husband and wife.

Still for you it seems impossible that the world can carry on

All that you can focus on is your grief, you're loved one's gone,

You feel anger and desperation, you are lost in your own world of grief

Still you cling to the one thing that will heal you and that is your belief.

And with that faith the day will come when you'll hear the birds sing again

The clouds will part and fade away with God's help from up in heaven.

"The darker the night, the brighter the stars, the deeper the grief, the closer is God."

~Fyodor Dostoevsky

Oblivion

You will never know how much I love you…loved you.

Only to have you reach in, grab my heart and rip it out of my chest.

Over and over like the relentless pounding of the ocean

To the shore with every wave.

Over and over again until I lay beaten

On the jagged shoreline of my emotions.

I eventually pick myself up tattered and bleeding.

I crawl into myself, thinking I'll never heal

Never forget the lashes of your tongue.

Slowly, painfully, I heal, and just when I'm able to breathe again

You hit me with another blow.

I fall stumbling, screaming no! Yet it continues.

I finally can fight you no more

To love someone so deeply is to lose. You won.

This time, let the crashing waves take me out to sea

And let me sink into oblivion.

For this is the end of my suffering

I am free, as is my love.

"If you never heal from what hurt you, you'll bleed on people who didn't cut you."
~Tamara Kulish

You Will Live

In this dark I try and see you
With my mind, you are my eyes
The pleading and cries surround me
As another soul says goodbye.

I reach out, "oh please can you hear me?"
"This just has to be a dream."
Then the black of night goes silent
With it takes the screams.

I'm unable to move
I am frozen in time
It's so dark
I can barely breathe.

I'm all alone in the blackness
"Are you there?"
"God please don't leave."

The clock stands still
Each second like an eternity,
"Please take away this wretched pain
Please come and rescue me."

Then through the blinds a glimmer of hope
As the sun's rays slice through the night.
For the first time in countless days
There is hope within my sights.

I feel a calm wash over me
The long shadows now disappear.
Then your voice speaks warm and gentle,
"Never doubt, I was always here".

"In your darkest moments
As you fought, I was right there holding your hand".
"As you fought I too was battling
Against the dark I took a stand".

"You came through the valley of shadows
You were brave and strong, stayed true".
"You will live, I have great plans for you,
I'm your God and I'll always love you".

"For the battle is not yours, it's Gods"
~2 Chronicles 20:15

Divine Intervention

The hours had no meaning, the minutes seemed like days

The seconds, each one eternity, as my life was slipping away.

My body shakes in agony as the shadows grow longer in my room

"Fight," He tells me, "Don't let it win." I sigh and feel I am doomed.

The air is thick and heavy as I struggle to take a breath

Too weak, and satan is laughing, "This will surely be your death."

In the gap between heaven and hell, I see a sliver of light through the black

I feel a force reach through the abyss, in that instant it pulled me back.

I gasped at the sight now surrounding me, dark shadows transformed to light

I felt such a calm come over me, I was given back my sight.

The darkness, the demons released me, now angels filled my room.

God, thank you for your divine intervention, you saved me from impending doom.

"Good will always triumph over evil because light will always overcome darkness."

~T. Hincks

Beautiful Flame

It's two years ago today that I got the call

The one we all dread, the worst one of all.

I was going to come see you as soon as I could

Just like I promised, I told you I would.

I tried to get to you, but you didn't wait.

The next day it came, but by then it was too late.

You were tired so God came and took you home

Now I'm left here to wander without you, on my own.

I'm trying to be strong, you didn't want me to be sad

"When I go, please don't cry." Can't keep that promise dad.

My chest hurts so deeply, I can't stand this pain

I'm just so distraught I won't see you again.

How do I live my life without you?

Now what am I supposed to do?

You were always there with a warm hug and a kiss

Your soft hand and blue eyes I so desperately miss.

I am honored to be your daughter, dad.

You were the best father a girl could ever have.

I never could have imagined such horrible pain

I'm cold and afraid, standing alone in the rain.

This world has lost another bright, beautiful flame

But heaven's much brighter, it's where I'll see you again.

A Blessing with Four Paws

They tell you not to cry, that he's just a dog.

Just a dog, not a human.

They tell you time will heal

That animals do not have emotions.

They didn't know that my dog was the only one

Who never left my side.

They don't know that the only one who hasn't judged me

And loved me unconditionally was my dog.

They don't know how scared I was

The night his moans and pacing woke me up.

They don't know my dog always slept beside me.

They don't know how much my dog enriched my life every day.

They don't know how many times I laid with him

And comforted him when he was sick.

They don't know how many times I noticed him limping

And his muzzle turning white.

They don't know how many times I talked to my dog

Cried with and laughed with my dog.

He was the only one who really listened.

They don't know how good I was to my dog

My dog was the only one who could sense

When I was ill, or in pain, or afraid.

They don't know what it's like to see your old dog

Trying to come over and say hello.

When things go wrong

My dog was always there, my best friend

Who loved me unconditionally.

They don't know that my dog trusted me completely

Every moment of his life, right up to his very last breath.

They don't know that I made a promise

To give him the best life

And that when his time came to cross the rainbow bridge,

I was there with him, stroking his soft fur

Kissing his face, whispering his name and, "I love you".

They don't know this ache in my heart is always there

And that the void he left in my life will never go away.

He wasn't just a dog.

He was my dog!

"I love you Monty, run free, and rest easy. My heart will always wear the pawprints left by you..."

You Threw Us Away

I still remember that summer day

When you took off your ring and threw it all away.

You made a promise, you took a vow

For better or worse, but look at us now.

Over half my life I walked by your side

With each passing day, a little more of me died.

You spiraled and sank into a hole so black

Desperately I tried to get you to come back

Days turned to months, I was a ghost to you

I tried so hard, there was no more I could do.

To you I was invisible, I felt so alone.

Yearning to once again have a loving home.

But fate wouldn't have it, you chose to look the other way.

After a lifetime together you threw "us" away.

"It's better to be alone than to be with someone who makes you feel alone."

Your Conscience

There's no where you can run or hide from your conscience.

It follows you, relentlessly. It stalks you. When you want sleep to come, when you need peace, quiet, and rest, your conscience doesn't allow it. It beckons you, eats at you, in the dark corners of your mind sleep defies you.

You battle with it as you toss and turn, sigh and weep, but to no avail will it leave you in peace.

For it knows the truth, and until the truth is set free it will haunt you, seek you out and follow you all the days of your life. You can't bury it, for where it is buried, deep in the dark shadows of your mind, there lies the guilt.

Guilt fuels your subconscious. It makes you ill. Like a cancer it festers from the years of hatred, deceit, and judgement. It consumes you like a two headed snake.

Oh how the demons delight in your guilty conscience. Where you should have said you're sorry but didn't. That place in your soul where you took rather than gave. The time you should have walked in another's shoes before you judged.

What can you do? What must you do to clear your mind from the relentless stalker of your thoughts?

You can run, you can hide. You can even pretend that nothing happened. Surely it will cease to bother you, and you will be at peace.

No my friend. Clear your mind of all the untruths…the lies…and wrongdoings. Pray, repent, ask for forgiveness. You will then, by the grace of God be blessed, forgiven, and have a clear conscience.

Darkness will turn to light, the shadows will retreat, and your conscience will be set free.

"Your Conscience is your judge in the court of your heart."

The Day of Reckoning

He created every single thing on earth.

Human, animals, things that creep and crawl.

Day and night. The sun, moon, stars. The Northern Lights that dance in the sky at night.

Seas, oceans, rivers and lakes.

The trees and plants of every kind.

The wind, rain and snow. The four seasons.

All He asked is that we take care of what He created.

That we love this earth as much as He does.

Look around you…what do you see?

Are you taking care of His creations?

He is watching. Will you be able to stand before Him with your head held high?

Or will you bow your head in disgrace?

The day of reckoning will come.

About the Author

Anna Marian Lachman grew up on a dairy farm just outside of Nisku, a quaint hamlet nestled in the heart of Alberta, Canada. Her childhood amidst nature and animals instilled in her a deep appreciation for the beauty of the four seasons, and wildlife. From an early age, Anna sensed emotions and connections others often overlooked, eventually recognizing herself as an empath. Writing became her conduit for channeling these profound feelings.

Life, for Anna, has been a tapestry woven with moments of joy, but also punctuated by regrets, mistakes, heartaches, and trials. She has known the depths of love and endured the pain of loss, bidding farewell to cherished loved ones and beloved pets. Yet, through it all, she has persevered, drawing strength from her faith and the unwavering support of her family, and friends.

Anna is blessed with her loving parents, four devoted brothers, a beautiful daughter, and two precious grandchildren who are the light of her life. Her journey took an unexpected turn in 2011 when she was diagnosed with Stage III Colon cancer. It was a pivotal moment, shaking her world to its core. But with unwavering resolve and steadfast faith, she embarked on a 10-year battle for her life. Today, Anna stands as a beacon of hope, having emerged victorious over cancer for 12 years now.

Throughout her trials, Anna's faith has been her guiding light. She credits her survival to her belief in God's plan and the strength that comes from trusting in His divine wisdom. To those facing their own struggles, she offers words of encouragement:

> "Hold onto faith, believe in the power of resilience, and trust that even in the darkest of times, light will eventually pierce through."

Anna's journey has been one defined by the full spectrum of human emotion—love, loss, faith, and triumph. In her book, she invites readers to walk alongside her, experiencing the depth and breadth of these emotions. Whether you've loved deeply, suffered loss, battled illness, or found solace in family bonds, Anna's words resonate with the universal truths that bind us all together. Each day, she reminds us, is a precious gift—a reminder of God's grace and the resilience of the human spirit.